PHOENIX FEATHER BOOKSELLERS

AND

LIBRARY BUSINESS PLAN

AND

ACADEMY CHAIN CONSERVATISM POLICY GUIDE

LEON LOWE

ISBN: Softcover   978-1-9845-4642-5
         EBook   978-1-9845-4641-8

Print information available on the last page

Rev. date: 08/09/2018

To order additional copies of this book, contact:
Xlibris
1-888-795-4274
www.Xlibris.com
Orders@Xlibris.com

PHOENIX FEATHER BOOKSELLERS AND LIBRARY BUSINESS PLAN AND ACADEMY CHAIN CONSERVATISM POLICY GUIDE

INTRODUCTION

Phoenix Feather Booksellers is a preface company to Phoenix Feather Youth Book Club. The purpose of this company is to build a portfolio of books and to sell them online independently.

Executive Summary

Ninarphay Tales is a series of children's novels designed to teach and instill morals and values through allegorized instances. What children learn in their youth echoes into their personality and status later on in life if shown that immoral indecency only gets them nowhere while moral decency gets you somewhere they are likely to follow that path. In each book, there will be a strong emphasis on virtue and morals over vice and indecency teaching and learning of the ways of Ninarphaians in a fantasyland.

In this book, four young women are rescued from an underworld realm called Transzalore, which is thwarted with evil monsters and dark lords. They learn that the realm of Ninarphay is built on harmony and virtue, and the harmonious virtues are kept in place by remaining consonant to good values and a moralistic nature. They also so learn that if ever the virtues of Ninarphay are Broken, the evil underworld will then gain leverage and claim their kingdom. Ninarphay is a magical kingdom realm filled with magical creatures and special ways of life. *Ninarphay Tales* are for the youth and the young at heart.

I am proposing to set up a youth book club across libraries for schoolchildren between eight to nineteen. A book club for the local youth of Kent is an enterprise scheme that is needed and most vital to a child's growth and mental enjoyment. This book club will encourage reading and an active interest in books and literature. The benefits of a book club on young children and teens are as follows:

A book club will

- keep the youth preoccupied and out of trouble;
- install values, morals, and ethics;
- get the youth actively interested in literary pursuits;
- provide a break from mundane stresses; and
- increase productivity and vocation to read books.

I am hoping to set up a book reading session fee of £2 and book purchase fee of £5, totaling £7 per recipient. These will be set out on permission slips given to schools and then from the schools to the school children. The permission slip will include the name of child, the name of parents, the parents' phone number, and the school's address.

From each £7 admission made, 20 percent will go to the local council and library, and 60 percent will go to the staff, an overall 8 percent will go to me, and the rest go to fund the company and employees' wages. The plan is to charge school recipients a £2 reading fee and £5 for a book, totalling £7. The reading periods will last thirty minutes to three-quarters of an hour, and then they will leave with the book that had been read to them and deposited for.

During the week, the school will be very busy and productive. An after-school club held five days a week on class rota, entertaining children for half an hour will do them good. This is a good deal and 20 percent to the local council and library could be a lot, depending on how much books are sold at the time of admission.

Twenty percent to further enhance council wealth and for an emergency school levy to build, restore, or enhance school classrooms.

The hope is to get thirty–sixty youths read for an hour, between 3:30 p.m. and 4:30 p.m. after school. If we reach this target, that would be fifty youth a day paying a total of £100 a day. If this trend lasts for days £500, a week £2000 for four weeks that would be £18,000 a term imagine rolling this across each school in Kent including every school yearly. In theory, that could make a profit of 11,700,000 in a school year. If Phoenix takes 20 percent profit, that's £2.340.000 a year to the local economy and four hundred additional staff on a salary of over £17.500 paid as daily commission.

I will employ one reader per school; this will take away an average of 70 percent from the school's daily commission.

Twenty percent in annual profit will go to Phoenix for the funding of schools and emergency projects. That's an extra 2.4 million a year, depending on how well the book club does. Seventy percent will go to employee wages that will be paid on commission. I will take 8 percent from the annual profit while my book sales will provide remuneration and royalty dividends.

Extracurricular activities, such as reading, not only provides a productive break, which leads to enhanced cognitive mental development and added brain capacity but also provides the school youth much needed mental stimulation and also a lot of personal fun that aides learning.

My books are written with the writing style of allegory, which means learning the difference between right and wrong, so when reading my book, the youth will always learn a valuable lesson between the differences of vice and virtue.

Each book provides attainment of morals, values, and ethics. In each of these books, the youth are taught the meaning of justice, honor, fortitude, grace, and morals. They are also shown instances of what greed, vice, disrespect, cruelty, and pride will and can bring.

These books are fun to read and provides much needed mental stimulation. The books are colorful to look at with pictures and illustrated backgrounds. These books expand moral mindfulness and social intelligence succinct and innocuously.

From the £7, 20 percent will go to the council in order to set up a countywide school levy for schools in the county under KCC. Order forms will be provided along with permission slips to ensure each youth receives their books accordingly.

There are 650 schools in Kent, each with an average a thousand student/pupils collectively. Phoenix Feather Youth Book Club intends to tap into this market and benefit the community as a whole by releasing funds to the economy and to the council. Providing the youth with a moral compass is another way we are benefiting and providing the youth with a moral compass is another way we are benefiting the community by installing values into the young of the community by installing values into the young.

Until I have built my portfolio of ten books (expected by spring), I will sell my books online on Amazon for £10 a unit. It will cost £4.80 to manufacture one book. One thousand units will cost £4,800, depreciation £10,000 in gross profits, £6,200 in net profits.

50.000 units, £24.000 depreciation, £100.000 gross profits, £76.000 net profits. £100.000 units, 48.000 depreciation £200.000 gross profits, £152.000 net profits.

1
Phoenix Feather Book Club

Phoenix Feather is a book club dedicated to the cognitive well-being and reading development of school children. I am a writer and entrepreneur who has researched many subjects over the years, including martial arts, health and medical care, criminal law, business, politics, and media.

My passion is writing, and I am preparing to write forty fantasy books called *Ninarphay Tales* in six months. Each book will be thirty–fifty pages long and takes around thirty–forty-five minutes to read. These books are children's books that bestow greater knowledge of moral value to the reader taking allegorized instances and mixing them with kingdom fairy tales, mythical creatures, fantasy characters, noble quests, sacred ornaments, and colorful texts. I would like to set up a youth book club to instill values, ethics, morals, and a sense of decency into the minds and ways of youth.

After reading this book, the youth will learn the monetary of value of kingdom, why you must listen to your elders and those in esteemed and reliable positions, to conduct yourself socially, the morals of justice, the power of sharing, why you shouldn't be tempted and generally doing the right thing.

- Book club for youth teaching allegory
- Keep the youth preoccupied and out of trouble
- Instill values, morals, and ethics
- Get the youth actively interested in literary pursuits
- Provide a break from mundane stresses
- Increase productivity and vocation to read books

Target market
- 130,000 school children in Kent County Council
- an appealing and entertaining book
- cheaper than online 15.99 – 5 pounds

My target market is parents who want the best for their children. This book is a loving fairy tale fantasy to read to school kids at night. *Ninarphay Tales* is a series of entertaining books that gives reading a stronger perspective on allegorized instances, a book that teaches and instills community, social values and ethics.

- School parents
- School kids
- Head teachers

Competitors
Competition is lax and there are already free after-school book clubs that offer free service in schools, but they don't offer a product and a unique service.

Our USP is allegorical, multistrand, new wave books that both entertain and hold value to the young and old minds alike.

Marketing and promotion service.

We offer a subscription service that caters to school children bestowing a book reading with fun and superfluous language that engages cognitive development on a semantic level.

Features of product
- Full color illustrated picture books
- Allegorical scenarios teaching youth wrong from right
- An entertaining fairy tale fantasy book
- An inclusive paid-for book each month
- An enjoyable reading experience

Benefit to customers
- Our customers get a bedtime story
- An inquisitively entertained child
- A child shielded from the mind-set of immorality and indecency

Methods to reach customers
- Hold in-school talks in schools with parents
- Hold in-school talks in schools with head teachers
- Provide order forms

How these will be achieved
- Contact schools through local council
- Persuade schools to sign our youth club contract
- Write powerful and evoking books that hold the customers' interest

2
Pricing and Costing

I.   Selling price per session £7
II.   On monthly subscription £22
III. £5 for a book £2 book reading fee
IV.   Per book is £15.99 with a £11.99 to £9.99 discount
V.   Competitors charge for service but don't provide a succinct exclusive product

Sales forecast

1. 130.000 school children
2. 650 schools
3. **£7 per session per child**
4. Nine-month contractual sessions per school lasting one week for each book
5. One hundred school children a month paying £7 a weekly session equals £700 a week, £2,400 a month across 650 schools equals £1,560,000 for over nine months equal £14,040,000

   Year 1 figures based on 100 primary schools with 300 pupils.
   Month 1 – 300+15 = 4500 + 100 = £450.000
   Month 2 – 300+15 = 4500 + 100 = £450.000
   Month 3 – 300+15 = 4500 + 100 = £450.000
   Month 4 – 300+15 = 4500 + 100 = £450.000
   Month 5 – 300+15 = 4500 + 100 = £450.000
   Month 6 – 300+15 = 4500 + 100 = £450.000
   Month 7 – 300+15 = 4500 + 100 = £450.000
   Month 8 – 300+15 = 4500 + 100 = £450.000
   Month 9 – 300+15 = 4500 + 100 = £450.000
   Month 10 - 300+15 = 4500 + 100 = £450.000
   Net profit £4.500.000 wages 80%

   Phoenix Feather booksellers

3
Executive Summary

Children's books are the most popular book type on the market with a broad range of consumers. Parents from every background and social type purchase these forms of books. One-fifth of the book market sales are from children's books, as over one-fifth are parents and the rest relatives at Christmas 1/3 of the book market belong to children's books.

Throughout the rest of the year, one-fifth of market sales in books belongs to the children's market. Children's books, when done right, are the most ethical, sustainable form of books in the book market as they fall into the timeless bracket of book genre at best.

Timeless means harmonious longevity of a book title and is known as the most sincere form of storytelling. In other words, children's books stick in the mind and stay with you longer when read as a child or teenager.

The *Ninarphay Tales* is a series of books that are timeless as they are engaging, metaphorical, entertaining, and educational. I believe that with the correct marketing, it can sell in the millions over the next year and be popular among all book readers. These books fall in the timeless bracket of storytelling.

Phoenix Feather booksellers is the preface business to Phoenix Feather Youth Book Club, and after many more books have been written and sold, Phoenix Feather Youth Book Club will open. This will be around a year after booksellers have been selling and there is enough money to fund the Phoenix Feather Youth Book Club.

Goals, aims, objectives

The goal of the Phoenix Feather booksellers is to buy author copies of *Ninarphay Tales* at 70 percent of RRP and sell them on Amazon with a markup. As this is my product, I am able to get a discount on each unit and sell them at the retail price or close to the retail price.

On Amazon, you can make additional sales profit of 20 percent product on product or a 10 percent loss of profits of over 50 percent depending on rates, VAT and seller's fees. In other words, I can earn up to 90 percent in profits or 50 percent in profits depending on sellers' fees and VAT. If sold at the full price, I could be set to make 90 percent in profits, and if sold at standard rate, just 50 percent in profits.

Market research

The children's book market is booming. There shouldn't be a problem selling books as children's books are the most popular books sold on the book market. Just look at J. K. Rowling and J. R. R. Tolkien, children's fairy tale fantasy authors both worth billions.

Target market

The target market of children's books is over one-fifth of the book market, and come Christmas, this jumps to a third. The children's book market is very lucrative and productive; this is an enterprising business to get into and can be deemed full proof as the fantasy children's book market has the strongest following. My book is available in over seventy countries and languages as it stands.

Features of product

The book will be a fully illustrated picture book with illustrated designed background layouts and illustrated designs of characters and locations. They are picture books with designs on each and every page of the book.

Each tale will convey and narrate an allegorical scenario with fresh, euphoric telling of allegorical instances. This book also uses the style of allegory to teach the youth wrong from right in a showdown of morals and perfect attitudes.

Allegory is a literal writing style that basically means being taught wrong from right. In *Ninarphay Tales* you see fantasy characters coming to terms with and taking decisions on what's wrong from right and facing the substantial consequences of their decisions and choices.

Ninarphay Tales offer to teach children wrong from right by entertaining light heartedly and with superfluous notion. All in all, *Ninarphay Tales* is the most enjoyable reading experience that gets to the heart of an intriguing and, at times, cavalier and magical situation.

This is the type of book you could read one hundred times to try and not miss a trick.

Benefits to customers

Bedtime story for kids and a child entertained and shielded.

The benefit of these books are that these are timeless bedtime stories for kids, young adults, and adults alike who would like to be transported to a magical kingdom before sleep. These books also benefit children by shielding them from contempt, vice, and unruliness.

Methods to reach customers

- Advertise on Amazon
- Set up a Facebook fan page
- Advertise on other social networking sites

> **Financial forecast for Phoenix Feather Booksellers Year 1**
> Month 1 - £25.000 = 5000 units = £10 a unit =£50.000
> Month 2 - 25.000 = 5000 units = £10 a unit =£50.000
> Month 3 - 25.000 = 5000 units = £10 a unit =£50.000
> Month 4 – £50.000 = 10000 units = £10 a unit = £100.000
> Month 5 - £50.000 = 10000 units = £10 a unit = £100.000
> Month 6 – £100.000 = 20.000 units = £10 a unit = £200.000
> Month 7 - £100.000 = 20.000 units = £10 a unit = £200.000
> Month 8 £250.00 = 50.000 units = £10 a unit = £500.000
> Month 9 – £250.00 = 50.000 units = £10 a unit = £500.000

Month 10 – £250.00 = 50.000 units = £10 a unit = £500.000
Month 11 – £500.000 = 100.000 units = £10 a unit = £1.000.000
Month 12 - £500.000 = 100.000 units = £10 a unit = £1.000.000
Net profit £4.250.000 units sold 425.000 gross profit £2.125.000
Overall profit £8.75 m

Pricing and costing
£11–£10.55 - £15.70 depreciation £4.80 – profit 11.90 -70% profit
£15–£13.86 - £19.01 depreciation £4.80 – profit £14.81 -100% profit

Each book will cost £4.80 to produce when sold on the will be sold for standard rate of £11 or the markup rate of £15. If sold at a marked up rate, I could make a ten-pound profit for each book. At the standard rate, only £7.10 a 65–70% profit.

Total amount needed: £15.000

Introduction
The purpose of this business guide is to outline targets for the next twelve months of business.
Music is a new wave tool used to enhance stimulation and entertainment. A record label is unique to other sectors and industries due to its work ethic and multimedia roots.
The goal of music is to appeal to the mass market and instill both mood and message.
In comparison with musicians and genres, all artists must strive to make positive and mainstream music where possible as other artist may make underground sub-experimental music. Mainstream artists must always appeal to the wider family market.
Music has a unique selling proposition, which comes in the form of multiple entertainments not previously done by a record label.
Each album released by artists must feature music, music videos, short film, documentary, artist biography/interviews, talent promos, and show reels.

Due to new wave and unique work ethic as well as high levels of creativity, the market opportunity is high and likely to dwarf other record labels.

In the company, there will be an executive board/committee made up of twelve representatives (staff).

Positions are to include business affairs correspondent, who will be in charge of payroll, bookkeeping, and label finances.

The legal officer will take care and oversee contracts and other legal responsibilities.

The A and R scouts for and guides talent.

The artists themselves will make music and various other projects.

The art and graphic design department will design logos for album covers and help with the advertising.

Marketing compiles and researches a marketing plan and also coordinates promotions and publicity to boost sales.

The publisher contacts journalists for reviews, interviews, magazines and newspapers on behalf of the artist and organizes broadcasting, web designs, or distribute sales.

The media department works on music videos, biography interviews, documentaries, short films, and various multimedia vocations.

Sales works on overseas relations, contacts record stores and retailers and ensures distribution.

The promoter secures radio airplay on the Internet and digital radio, arranges gigs and tours, keeps in constant contact with other departments and committee members.

Artist development reviews contracts and career plans with artist, gets involved with marketing and promotion, solicits videos to music stations.

Staffing

Chief executive officer – ensures the company is fulfilling targets and strategies.

Managing director – reviews company initiatives and strategies, setting targets for relevant committee members.

Business manager – looks after and reviews label finances, bookkeeping, and payroll.

Legal officer – takes care of contracts and legal responsibilities.

Artist and repertoire – locates and signs talent, helps with song selection and selection of producer, communicates with business manager, and ensuring paperwork and accounting are set up properly.

Art director – product design, CD cover, trade, consumer press, advertising, retail sales, posters and print media.

Marketing – the marketing department is responsible for the overall marketing plan, coordinates the promotion and publicity of an artist and runs a sales campaign.

Publicity – arranges feature stories for TV shows and various media-related themes, such as interviews; record reviews; web broadcast; radio; local, national, international newspapers and magazines.

Media – produces and promotes music videos, overseas promotion and marketing, review web-based opportunities. The head of media will usual scout for a production crew.

Sales – oversees retail activity, contracts with record stores, distribution of product, the promotion and publicity at the record label.

Promotion - secures radio airplay on the Internet, national and international radio stations. The promoter constantly communicates with all other departments.

Artist development – develops career plan of artist, coordinates marketing and promotion, solicits videos to music stations.

Producers/Music Engineers/Ghost Writers/Artists
Financial Projections
Performance fees
Interviews

Record Label Recording Contracts Requirements
Publishing Income Resources
Ringtones, audio streaming, mechanical royalties, performance royalties, sheet music sales, commercials/jingles.
Artist Expenses

Recording fees, CD producer/engineer, studio costs, CD/digital stage costs, studio equipment, graphic artist cover and design, CD manufacturing duplicate charges, promotional expenses—radio/sales rep marketing sales cost.

Publicity/Promotion Costs

Publicists/publication fees, promo/publicity kit design, flyers, posters, advertising costs, printing/copying charges.

Photographer fees, duplication charges; website design and maintenance charges; access fees; bills: Internet, phone lines, fax, tax, and booking fees.

Equipment Costs

Tour luggage, equipment (musical instruments/keyboards), CDs/MP3s (for listening studying) sound system, rehearsal space costs (arena/stage).

Music Production

Song writing – copywriter costs, performance rights, operation fees.

Artist, Business Team Costs

Personal management, consultant's fees, business manager, accountant fees, booking agent fees, publicity fees.

Transportation Costs

Bus purchase, maintenance costs, airline, train, ferry.

Merchandize

T-shirts etc., design costs, manufacturing costs.

Miscellaneous Expenses

Stage clothing, insurance, trade magazine subscription costs.

4
Business Objectives

Innovation Blaze Music, a record label with unique and entertaining features that will be brought to a worldwide audience. On the full release of each album, there will be an entertainment montage each with a unique and well-groomed theme.

This montage will include artist biography, short film, music videos, documentaries and style talent demos. (This is also a unique selling proposition.)

Within the first month of fire arts launch, I will have employed an executive committee consisting of twelve key members who will, at first, head departments in their chosen fields.

I would have found roughly ten individual artists who I will then brief on specific assignments and on how I want their music to sound. I will spend time with them personally to improve, develop, and diversify their skills. Then I will begin work on music production/engineering, getting the sounds right that all people would like to hear it. We will begin recording and networking for the artist's promotion.

In the second month of fire arts launch artist development will receive instructions to edit through the musicians music to ensure that subversive standards and clean content is being met. (Content control)

The media department will select a few, if not all, of the songs for music videos. Once the videos have been shot, they will be marketed to the relevant TV stations.

Marketing Sales Distribution
Blaze Music will promote artists through radio, TV, and web interviews. A sleek marketing campaign will be held promoting fire art artists through various publicity and advertising schemes.

Blaze Music will encourage artists and aim to target a wide and varied audience diversifying and initializing innovative music.

Blaze Music will market and advertise a wide range of media products through album sales. Products include artist's style talent demo, short films, music videos, artist's biography and interviews, documentaries, and most importantly, music.

What's appealing about fire art is its subversive, innovative image with creative multifaceted media and iconic role models audiences everywhere will be allured.

The price of a Blaze Music's multimedia album will range at thirty–forty pounds, but if the retailers and professional marketers ebb down, we will follow suit. For a separate album with only music, the retail price will be ten pounds.

The annual turnover per album is expected to range in at between ten– forty million pounds, of which the company gets 25 percent.

Marketing Strategy – The marketing department will work with the media department and publicity department to advertise on television via commercials and chat shows, interviews, as well as on radio and billboards.

The marketing department will then work with the business manager and sales department to arrange for product placement in retail stores. Fire art will set up a special website exclusive to fire art and its multimedia products. This website will be advertised on the television.

Blaze Music will have a keen focus on creating jobs in the urban media entertainment sector. Also, artists will be asked to become an album sponsors and to invest in further projects.

Lyricism
In order to make money from music, you must have lyrics, and the only way to get lyrics is to learn how to write. Every lyric ever made has been a

meditation. Music is rarely about impression or materialism; music is all about expression and reflection.

Expression is the need to teach either lifestyle or persona. Reflection is a core meditative technique that provokes thought of a shadowed situation. It is an insinuation, a sensibility or a repelled curse.

Lyricism in music is not about impression in any way and never should a lyricist or songwriter get confused for a bearer of impression.

In order to write lyrics, you must have a reason to write. There is no writing of lyrics without depth of thought and inner reflection. When writing your lyrics, you must remember the importance of being infuse hobbies, passions, feelings.

Concepts of words – How is a word bought to life, why is a word bought to life, what does that word mean, why does that word have that meaning?

Spoken word – What effect does that word have on listeners? Why should listeners listen to that word? What does that word mean to the listeners?

Biology of words – How is a word made up? What does that word bring to the soul of listeners? How does that word make you feel? Is it in the correct context?

Represented detail – How often does this word occur in lifestyle settings? What does this word bring to a lifestyle setting? Why does this word bring this to a lifestyle setting? Why have you chosen that?

Philosophical impact – How will your music benefit the future of cultural generations? What tradition of music does your word belong to? Why will this benefit humanity and why? Will your music corrupt or define?

Creation of Acoustics

In order to set up a record label, you are going to need a small studio with equipment. It couldn't be simpler. The studio does not have to be larger than

25m2, but it must be larger than 20m2. If you are one of the lucky ones, you can find or create a studio in your home or conspire with a close relative and friend or a distant relative and friend.

Once you find a place for the studios, you must find enough money to put together a proper studio. A proper studio consists of at least four microphones costing around one hundred great British pounds each and a fully functioning sound system and sound booth. The collective costs, including the first year's electricity bill could be up to fifty thousand British pounds.

Different sources of music have different connotations, creating different sounds. A jingle is created by tapping together two pieces of metal slowly and efficiently. A chime is created when clashing metals are rattled together. A gong is created when a padded stick is hit vivaciously against a hollow precious metal. A sound is made naturally by the wind and can be used as music. A bass sound is created by to large depth filled instruments clashing with strength and speed, usually at a slow rate.

5
Academic Education

Academics is a learning style more distinct and more efficient than any others. Academics involves prolific study of all or any given subject underlying and reinforcing each key point and dissertation of each key point.

There are five main criteria of an academy, the first one being, principal admission. An academy's principal must govern all aspects of an academy and subsequent chairs. A principal must ensure all pupils in attendance must comply with the relevant criteria related to that particular academy, i.e., sport, history and philosophy, creative arts, etc.

The second charge is the bookkeeper. A bookkeeper is the deputy of a principal academic chain. The bookkeeper's role is to log and file relevant records of pupils and events. A bookkeeper is the principal librarian of an academy chain and must section, file, generate, and enumerate relevant events in chronological order. This must happen in the way of qualification level and accreditation percentage.

The third principle of an academy chain is the caretaker chief. The caretaker chief must take care and look after the upkeep of any given academy that they are assigned to as the first chieftain principle.

The caretaker chief must review and verify the relevance of all and any articles in importance and development.

E.G local of keys, pupils, articles and assignment, the training and planning of staff, the continuity and practicality of property and all out safety, security, discipline and sensibility of justice and cohesion.

The fourth charge are the janitor, inspector, surveyor. The inspectorate surveyor is the highest ranking aficionado who works the most hours. The contractual duty of the janitor inspectorate surveyor is to review and record logged events, update registrations and records, allocate vocation to the correct ward.

Final principle aspect – chief principal examiner, clearances, grading, awards, examinations, and allocations.

The chief principal examiner is the final principle of an academy and is usually only present at grading, admissions, and office surgeries.

The chief principal examiner's mission is to assess, review, and remark on the attributes of pupils and students.

Academic education is all about intensive study, further study and accreditation allocation. Full academic education does not begin until the vocation of a basic education has an advanced merit. A basic education consists of seven modules of key stages 1, 2, and 3. These modules include, history, geography, math, science, English, art, and finally, life skills.

The full entry to academic education begins at thirteen and goes on until twenty-five where a first foundation degree is key base and highest award.

The legal limit for students in academics is twenty-one. After the first diploma, there is a final academic course where the student can then soon earn a first foundation degree up to level 5 masters. Then the student will have the choice to carry on for a PhD at the university level or apply for vocation.

An academic college must display three inexplicable by-laws absolute discipline, the studiousness to remain quiet in class and in the library as well as keeping self to self and only speaking when spoken to.

Seclusion and distance, no fraternization or excessive socializing, studiousness and academia involves the willingness to study and achieve without constant gossiping and skivvying annoyance.

The third inexplicable rule of an academic chain is an academy must install and promote a cultured and composed base of parental guidance. This includes a definite dedication and underpinning devotion to child safety and well-being. That means no expressions of profanity, no stealing, or taking of work and property, no violations of decorum and adamant composures, no slanderous speeches or gossiping, no idle behavior and unusual circumstances.

There are many academic teaching styles, infant and primary academics begins and ends between the ages of seven–thirteen and largely involves literacy and numeracy as the key base curriculum.

All academy teachers and lecturers will be expected to keep to their allocated vocation at an academy. Teachers and lecturers will be preoccupied as administrators. This keeps the ideologue and representation of an academy business like and nationally important.

Teachers and lecturers will help with clothing and uniform, productivity and materials to be sold through the academy chain and on the regional market. Science tech is to be examined and improved where necessary as a means to underpinning and distinctly ascertaining wither or not the exploit product is efficient to be objectified and valid enough to be taught.

Geography tellurics are to be produced and stored for either personal use or to be sold on to another organization, this is the way academies make their principle finances. The library style of academics must incite, intrinsic bookkeeping, and qualification records board on a numeral semiotic system, level 1 basic–level 5 expert.

6

Diocese College Faith Academy of Productivity and Business

Intensive training three-month workshop diploma courses: One-off payment of 360 pounds for each workshop course taken over a three-month period where the candidate will receive a qualification after the three-month period:

Ten site buildings:
1. prayer cathedral: theology
2. agriculture and catering area
3. health science and social science area
4. creative arts area
5. hospitality, tourism and alternative therapy area business and accounting area
6. construction area
7. mechanical engineering area
8. technology and IT area
9. design, textiles and embroidery area

Unique selling propositions
1. academy college open to all learning types
2. short-term intensive training courses for GCSEs A levels, diplomas, and degrees
3. transparent grading system/qualified tutors, teachers, lecturers
4. free at the point of use until qualified and working except a small affordable one-off entry fee
5. work experience offered on extended campus plus links to industry
6. business is a mandatory subject when enrolling
7. the campus offers accommodation, permanent and temporary/

The surrounding area of the campus will be in a productivity village of differing sectors of industry and enterprise. The theology academy offers new businesses to begin and flourish. The church hall and community center will be used for prayer meetings, theological teachings, business meetings, and graduation ceremonies. The library will double as a booksellers and be a place to read, study, research, purchase and publish books via the academy. As the library will sell and publish books, we will use this as a way to subsidize further educational studies. There will be an on-site restaurant catering to the needs of students and tutors as well as visitors. We will also create childcare and housing facilities to help those who are in the social care system. There will be a leisure and hospitality spa on site for paying customers at the vicinity, as well as for students studying. These will be occupied for apprenticeships by the hospitality students. There will also be a retail mall and shopping park for the textiles and business students to work in as an apprenticeship. These sectors of education, creative arts, social care, catering, hospitality and leisure, and retail industry will surround and be owned by the academy and are for both public and private use. These retail consortiums are expected to generate vast profits for the academy and sustain our small, affordable one-off entry fee for all of our students. They will also increase local output by at least 10 percent. These industrial and academic zones will be in each county and city in the regions of the United Kingdom. They will each cater for a sector retrospectively: (1) creative arts, (2) healthcare and hospitality, (3) technology and renewable technology, (4) construction, (5) sociology, (6) catering and agriculture. These are the main industries and entrepreneurial sectors that will drive the local and national growth of the United Kingdom's GDP and its productivity.

Employment
Three tiers of tutelage, creative arts, GCSE, A level, tier 1, diploma foundation degree tier 2, degree, higher degree tier 3. Creative writing and media 3 tier 1, 3 tier 2, 4 tier 3. Performing arts 3 tier 1, 4 tier 2, 5 tier 3. Music and theology 4 tier 1, 4 tier 2, 5 tier 3. Digital art and illustration 4 tier 1, 4 tier 2, 5 tier 3. Digital and multimedia 3 tier 1, 4 tier 2, 3 tier 3.
qualifications.

GCSE, A level, Diploma Tier 1, Foundation Degree, Tier 2. Higher Degree Tier 3.

Three tiers of tutelage, creative arts, GCSE, A level, tier 1; diploma foundation degree, tier 2, degree, higher degree,tier 3. Alternative medicine, healthcare, social care and hospitality services. Health services 3 tier 1, 4 tier 2, 5 tier 3. Nursing and healthcare 3 tier 1, 4 tier 2, 5 tier 3. Hair and beauty (media) stylist 2 tier 2, 3 tier 2. Holistic therapy 3 tier 1, 4 tier 2, 5 tier 3. Holistic medicine 3 tier 1, 4 tier 2, 5 tier 3.

Three tiers of tutelage, creative arts, GCSE, A level, tier 1, diploma foundation degree tier 2, degree, higher degree tier 3. catering! Professional cookery 5 tier 1, 6 tier 2, 7 tier 3. Pastries confectionery, 2 tier 1, 3 tier 2, 4 tier 3. Hotel management 4 tier 1, 4 tier 2, 5 tier 3. Hospitality services 3 tier 1, 3 tier 2, 4 tier 4. Events management 1 tier 1, 2 tier 2, 3 tier 3. Hospitality supervision 2 tier 1, 2 tier 2, 3 tier 3.

Three tiers of tutelage, creative arts, GCSE, A level, tier 1, diploma foundation degree tier 2, degree, higher degree tier 3. Construction, technology, renewable technology and engineering. Bricklaying, painting, and decorating 6 tier 1, 6 tier 2, 6 tier 3. carpentry 3 tier 1, 3 tier 2, 3 tier 3. Plumbing 3 tier 3, 3 tier 2, 3 tier 3. Electrician 3 tier 1, 3 tier 2, 3 tier 3. Bench joinery, wood machinery 1 tier 1, 2 tier 2, 3 tier 3. Engineering and technology 3 tier 1, 4 tier 2, 5 tier 3. Mechanical and electrician 4 tier 1, 5 tier 2, 6 tier 3. Shipping and maritime 6 tier 1, 7 tier 2, 8 tier 3.

1. Campus 1: creative arts, 53 tutors for the five forms of creative arts.
2. Campus 2: alternative health and healthcare, 55 tutors.
3. Campus 3: 63 tutors for catering, hospitality and agriculture.
4. Campus 4: 101 tutors for construction, engineering and renewable technology.

GCSE A level pay: 30k – 17 tutors – £510.000 per annum
Diploma foundation degree pay: 54 k – 19 tutors – £1.026.000 per annum
Higher degree, PhD pay: 80 k – 24 tutors – £1.920.000 per annum

GCSE A level pay: 30 k – 14 tutors - £420.000 per annum
Diploma foundation degree pay: 54 k – 15 tutors – £810.000 per annum
Higher degree, PhD pay: 80 k – 20 tutors – £1.600.000 per annum

GCSE A level pay: 30 k – 17 tutors – £510.000 per annum
Diploma foundation degree pay: 54 k – 20 tutors – £1.080.000 per annum
Higher degree, PhD pay: 80 k – 26 tutors – £2.080.000 per annum

GCSE A level pay: 30 k – 30 tutors - £900.000 per annum
Diploma foundation degree pay: 54 k – 34 tutors – £1.836.000 per annum
Higher degree, PhD pay: 80 k – 37 tutors – £2.960.000 per annum

Staffing summary

1. Two to three tutors teaching in the same class at once.
2. Several classes each with a specified tutor, a vice tutor, and an assisting tutor.
3. Tutors will be expected to teach around two classes a day.
4. Tutors will have around five–six days full time, receiving either £20 per hour, £34 per hour, or £48 per hour.

Business summary

1. Increased enterprise, industry productivity, more high-powered, high-paid earners
2. More people learning and taking part in academic study and producing books (publishing, productivity).
3. An increased education sector with more access to degrees and easier access to higher education learning.
4. More flexible and trustworthy than the old tuition system, free at the point of use except for an affordable one-off entry fee.
5. Business planning lessons will be mandatory along with this many schemes to open up a new business at the end of study will be put to all of our candidates.
6. Increased business productivity.

7. Working with local councils, estate agents, and building houses near campus to look after housing accommodation needs.

Four campuses, each dedicated to a specified sector, including mandatory business and theological lessons with a church hall for meetings, graduation and ceremonies.

Campus 1 is dedicated to the creative sector; this includes, creative writing, performing arts, media, music and theology.

Campus 2 will be dedicated to the health and social care services sector; sociology, as well as physical anatomy and holistic and alternative therapies will be studied at degree and diploma levels.

Campus 3 will be dedicated to construction, renewable technology, technology and engineering.

Campus 4 will be dedicated to agriculture, catering, hospitality and leisure including retail.

Outside of these campuses, there will be public enterprise zones for local business endorsed with, Catering, fashion, technology, star up fairs for local business. The academy will also build housing, both permanent and temporary, for our students. This type of usage of the campus will boost productivity four fold in that area, contributing to local productivity. The theology hall will be open to the public on the weekend, and tithes will be offered to the local church strictly for church purposes. These academy colleges will be used to fast track higher education into forms of employment, business, apprenticeship and qualification. The plan is to get 100 percent of over twenty-one year olds into higher education, boosting all with the higher prospect of a good job and well-to-do staffing occupancy.

Business objectives
1. Each creative arts student is to publish a book as end-of-the-year assignment for those in the diploma level and upward. Each student

will be given 80 percent in royalties, and the rest will fund the academy. This will be one of the ways the academy makes its revenues and remunerations through sponsorship of in-house businesses.

2. Each business, catering, engineering and software student will be asked to complete a product design as an end-of-the-year assignment, which will then go on to the market for sale. This product will then become the student's first business project.

3. Each theology student will be asked to try and set up a church and community center that will become part of a larger network of churches in their local area. I'e daycare, kitchen, social care provider.

7

E-Commerce Guide to Education and Academics
Sovereignty Part 2: Business and E-Commerce

Introduction

A business embodies community livelihood and social functionality. A family-run business keeps the spirits of the towns and counties stable and contented. When people are occupied and active with skill, intelligible pursuits, and true talents, wholeness and well-being become their own reward.

The study of e-commerce pertains to the work and structure on a portended scale. Individuals who procrastinate and conform to the laws and rules of their elders and masters win and gain.

Business and e-commerce are the vocations of architecture and leisure. The way of a true professional credits the ways of code and conduct, implies the rules of law, endorses opportunities for staff of natural qualities and delegates arrangements of tasks and duties inherent on forms of application.

The only way to achieve merit in the realm of business is through qualification, application of rules and regulations and a concise consonance of maturity.

A real business is built on the foundation of legislation, the principle of accreditation and financial law, the temperance and value inherent in the outcome of contractual disputes, and the design and civil service of citizen rights.

Sovereign

Sovereignty pertains to how much a household, street, area, community, town, council, borough, county, city, region, state and country has to live on to fund communal essentials such as food, cloths, hygiene, shopping, stimulation, medicines, bills, household goods, tax and fuel.

The foundation essentials for a fully operational elder include household appliances, essential travel, business fees, sport and exercise, marriages and romance, child care and family well-being.

In order to gain independence, a citizen must produce commerce or conduct administrative authority. E-commerce reflects on industries and sectors and how they fair in terms of sales, quotas and consumer satisfaction.

The eight main sectors include the services sector, healthcare sector, creative sector, hospitality sector, financial sector, construction sector, manufacturing sector, and agricultural sector.

Economic governance refers to the way in which politicians and business leaders coordinate both theory systems and statistical analysts to define the viability and validity of a business enterprise.

The benefits of migrants working in a foreign country is good as long as ideals and culture is identical to our own. For example, Latin America, Russia, and Southeast Asia are island types and sovereign states.

Capital enterprise is the title given to a business which is sure to do extremely well and generate wealth. Capital enterprise companies can only earn this title if they meet these requirements: they have an essential product, supply and demand corresponds to their customs base, the product can make at least a 70 percent profit with each unit sold.

The purpose of a capital enterprise is to generate wealth for the employable community by the employable community.

Work and communal foundations: communal foundations in regard to UK culture and tradition is varied and far ranging. The United Kingdom's prime territories include Ireland, Scotland, Wales, and central England. Each have different ways of doing things unique to their personal identity.

Ireland, Scotland, and Wales's prime foundation relies on agriculture, farming, and distillery. These are the three most important traits of a country and regions' economic structure.

The UK, England, and Northwest France, as examples, rely heavily on services as its prime communal foundation.

A-F-D is the most important of all the sectors, as this is how we provide and nurture for ourselves.

The service sector includes social and medical care services, and when regional powers are disowned by certain services, social class systems and qualifications will be intruded to RC subcouncils to overlook all forms of communal foundations in that district.

A secure port of call for the United Kingdom are Italy, Greece, Spain, Portugal. The communal foundations of the countries vary, but the usual always involves some form of Catholicism.

Forms of parity compatibility include religion, cooking, health, clothing styles, and structure systems.

Tax and revenue: The importance of tax and revenue is that tax must be paid to the government's treasury in order to benefit the sovereign wealth fund, which is for the benefit of the commonwealth of custodians of the country. Paying tax to the government is a key principle for any hard-working citizen. Usually, the monies paid to the government is reused for beneficial communal causes, i.e., welfare benefits, medical care, town maintenance, educational foundations.

Ability and qualification: Work and awards must only be awarded to the correct people. People with high skill levels must always receive remuneration according to their skill, ability, quality, and productivity of work. Family businesses must always remain in the family, from kin to close relations. Those who fall out of this transient status must purchase.

Business and E-commerce

Business and e-commerce are the foundations of a thriving civilized society. The administration system of a business and the sovereign productivity of an e-commerce combine to bring order, structure, and definition to society.

There are five key components of business and e-commerce. These are productivity, efficiency, professionalism, education, and legislation.

Productivity entails promotion and endorsement of a public and or private working for the benefit and welfare of others with the end prospects of financial advancement.

There are four by-laws of productivity. These include production, supply and demand, distribution, and remuneration.

The second key component of productivity is efficiency. Efficiency entails hard work and determination. Without these two components. the idea of productivity is useless and wasted. There are three forms of efficiency: vocation, activity, and study.

The third component of business and E-commerce is professionalism. Professionalism entails clarity and idealism as a principled worker. There are four forms of professionalism. These are codes of conduct, delegation, contractual arrangements, and vested interest.

The fourth foundation component of business and e-commerce is education. It is important that the beneficiary of a company's administration is well-educated and 100 percent compliant of the rules and regulations of that companies order as stated on contract. There are three forms of education that must be adhered to and specified certification, company policy, and recorded marketing.

The fifth and final foundation component of business and e-commerce is legislation. Legislation is the most valuable foundation component of any e-commerce enterprise. Legislation implies law and order while upholding the moral sanctity of society. Legislation ensures that the rightful aspects of works and productivity are imparted to the responsible recipient. The three main aspects of legislation include financial law, contractual arrangements, and citizen rights.

8
Terms and Conditions

ARRIVAL

On Time – When employed by Wuning, you are expected to arrive on time for work every day in order to maintain composure and a keen body clock.

Daily – As a Wuning employee, you are expected to work five days a week, from Monday to Friday, and have the weekends of.

Eight Hours – The hours of work for a Wuning employee are eight hours, depending on department usually six days a week. After working ten weeks for eight hours a day and six days a week, you will be granted annual leave.

MEETINGS

Lecture Rooms/Screen Theaters – Meetings will take place often in lecture rooms and screen theaters.

Work Schedules – Work schedules will be handed out at these meetings that will discuss briefs projects and assignments drawn up and worked on for department use.

BEHAVIOR/MATURITY

Correspondence – Terms and conditions of working for Wuning is you will have to be correspondent in your approach to people and the relevant staff.

Responsible – Take responsibility for your department and yourself. Don't become irresponsible if something doesn't go your way or you're not persuaded.

Civilized – Your manners toward others are important, so always behave in a civilized toward yourself and others to maintain company composure.

Credible – If you find any member to be credible, then alert your superior to their suitability as this will keep up company tranquility.

Decent – You must always maintain a decency to yourself and the community don't let ego cloud your judgment and remain decadent to those who are relevant.

Cognizant – It is in Wuning Productions' best interest that the staff and employees remain cognizant of the situations that they endeavor.

MANNERISM

Sensible – When on site or within the premises, always reflect on your duty and remain sensible to the task and function on hand.

Self-controlled – Remain contained, calm, and focus when tackling issues and asserting yourself in your assignments. Assertion and temperament are vital for a healthy body and mind.

Calm – Being calm in every situation is a great point winner for the employment standards at Wuning. The calmer staff are at completing projects the better the airs.

Polite – Being polite to your seniors and staff member is an important thing to maintain decadence in the workplace. This will make everybody more at ease with everybody else.

Awake – Make sure every time you attend work, which you must do every day, you are bright eyed alert in the morning and bushy tailed ready to go.

CAUTIONS

Deduction – If a member of the staff is found violating the code of conduct or breaking the rules and regulations, they will receive a deduction in their salary.

Adhere – If a member of the staff doesn't adhere to what is being said to them, then they will be issued with a caution unless they can verify that they heard and rectified their mistake.

Respond – Responding to cautions is vital for the vacancy of staff and their overall counter to a caution.

Reappropriate – If the staff can reappropriate their caution or admission to an employee, then the caution will sooner be lifted.

Warning

Acquittal – Acquittal of contract will take place if company polices are not kept in check and employment suitability appropriately respected.

Probate – This means filing the first warning before a decision is made. At this time, employees will have enough time to put together a case, if not, an acquittal.

Ascertain – If problems occur and can't be ascertained due to lack of evidence, then an investigation will ensue throughout the company.

STAFF MEETINGS

Form/Formal – Staff meetings will be formed regularly. Attending will be formal for intended employees.

Correspond – In staff meetings, all employees will be expected to respond to what is being discussed?

Attend – It is important for employees to be present at these meetings to fulfill their tasks and duties accordingly; if not, they will be reviewed and dropped.

Liaise – At these staff meetings, they will have to liaise and mediate with each other and other staff members.

STAFF TRAINING

Vigorous, Frequent – Staff training will be vigorous and frequent. Everyone will have to attend and be alert as much as they're awake. Here is where you will understand the purpose of your task.

Responsibilities – During staff training seminars, employees will get their duties and responsibilities.

REPORTS

In-depth Daily – most of the work at Wuning will be in the form of one-page reports filled and annotated for a project or assignment.

Forecasts – forecasts of circumstances and events will be written in these reports and talked about over the phone and on the Internet.

Paperwork – formalities will be put to light when paperwork is written down so everybody will take form these sheets and put onto assignment.

Regular – reports will go out weekly for the use of managers and hierarchy so relevant articles are taken instead of massive documents.

Efficient – the articles will have to be made efficient and endearing so they are easy to read and understandable.

INDUCTIONS

On Entry – inductions will take place after contracts and application forms have been decided. After inductions have been admitted work will begin.

Reviewed analysis – inductions will be reviewed for analysis after the first three months of employment at Wuning.

Calendar regulation –

AUTHORIZATION

Staff Hierarchy
Employment
Decisive – To be employed by Wuning, you must have decisive flare, an intelligent outlook, and honorable stature.

Hard Work – when working for Wuning, you are expected to have a charismatic determination that leads to working hard in the building.

Rules and Regulations – follow and cooperate with the rules and regulations set out by the company in its policies or else face indefinite acquittal.

CODES HAVE CONDUCTS -

BRIEFS

Regular DISSERTIVE Handouts –
Projects –
Assignments –

All staff at Wuning Production Company are advised to read and follow the following instructions followed by the company's code of conduct policy carefully.

The staff and employees must take into account all that is written on the contract and abide by the rules and regulations set out by management to avoid disqualification and possible acquittal.

The statements read are to ensure that everybody works hard to an obedient standard and company decorum is maintained and secured.

When standards and targets are met, everyone will be a lot happier, at ease, and sociable with others.

At Wuning, the terms and conditions are kept for the convenience of the staff and employees to ensure that everybody is happy and contented with each other.

PRIVACY AGREEMENT

Security Cards – Security cards will be dispatched to employees with a chain to wear around the neck of staffs who will have access to main site.

These security cards must be worn at all times to ensure so that no articles go missing and that everything is kept in its place.

Liaison Meetings – No staff member are to discuss out of permission the business of a client's liaison meeting.

Frequent liaisons will be necessitated to take place on the premises for the individual purpose of staff and employees.

Code of Security – Files are to be kept locked in a safe and detached environment with a lock and key system.

Security staff are to keep an eye on the surroundings and ensure nothing illegal is taking place if otherwise report it.

Secretary Staff Training – All secretaries are not to tell anyone, apart from their assigned manager, of any talks and discussions as everything must be kept private.

Secretaries will have training sessions to ensure that they don't inform outsiders about any company dealings.

Files will be annotated and stored in a cabinet to ensure that company confidentiality is kept intact.

Staff-Only Rules – All staff is expected to inform each other of any relevant articles, and business information must be introduced to them in staff meetings. Only staff is allowed on site, and anyone without a security badge or who isn't staff must be escorted off the premises.

Rules and Regulations – Follow the instructions set by the senior of your department. Show restraint to all and other employees.

Treat others how you will expect to be treated. Refrain from unlawful conduct. Don't trouble any other staff with blasphemous or negative insults.

Travel Costs – Travel arrangements will first be handled by logistics. Register with administration before taking out any cash sums. Any unknown personnel will be expected to find their own way of travel. Apply to administration if you are planning a trip out of the country. Book the company coach if planning a project.

Surveillance Sheets – Draw up documents on assignments.
Record and report all goings and out takings used in company times. Evaluate hazards and risks while on assignment at all times. Keep a note of department goings on.
Security will have provisional use of surveillance.

Polite to Customers – Show a mild, modest form and astute demeanor toward the clientele. Inform the clientele of your project after the staff room has been alerted. Don't show clientele until contracts have been signed.

Security Badges – Wear security badges at all times. Acknowledge their use and employ it.

Privacy Agreement – Company Policies

Company Policies

Answer to Your Commanding Staff Member – Employees are expected to answer and cooperate with their superior staff member.

As a Wuning journalist, you are expected to follow the command of your seniors and do what you are told by your manager.

Management appraisal of the Wuning journalist, you will be assessed as to your history and have your next of kin notified at any circumstance.

Your manager will evaluate any needs that you have and ensure that you can settle in your post.

Wuning does not tend discrimination. You will not be likely to lose your vocation after assessments and evaluation.

Your manager will make a judgment of your needs such as salary, days off, rest bite and posted vocation. Wear decent attire at all times suit tie and comfortable shoes and casual cloths.

Be Polite to Members of the Staff – At Wuning, you are expected to show respect to all members of the staff. Stay within limits of stature and demeanor toward people.

Respect everyone you come into contact with in society. Form yourself with clarity and in decency.

Have a polite etiquette and adequacy in everything that you do while working for Wuning Productions.

Liaise with the Staff – The Wuning staffs are expected to mix and socialize diversely without prejudice with other staff.

Communicate competently at staff meetings. File the monthly reports and evaluate them at the end of the working month. A ten-page document every month minimal.

Discuss briefs among yourself and other staff members without becoming to attach or to withdraw.

When confident of the ability and personnel attributes file the relevant paperwork with the company to begin your independent projects.

Maintain Composure – Look after you're eating habits and dietary needs at all times and stay hydrated. If you are having personnel problems, consult a specialist.

For alternative difficulties alert a member of staff ascertain self-control and keep within limits of fact and reality. Do not imply or implicate on other people in anyway.

Keen focus when in the office or preparing for assignments. Stay sharp and have a keen focus for the task at hand.

Hold a respectable balance remain charmed and take efficiency into account when it comes to tasks and work-related topic.

Communicative charm, if unconvinced of your confidence or abilities reiterate yourself and make sure that you can hold a communication with clear, unchallenged speech to the best of your abilities. (Being literate is of abstinent importance at this level of media).

When arriving to work, make sure you glow with clarity and hygiene, so we know that you are maintaining your health and respecting others.

Adamant temperament, if a situation is getting to you or you feel under pressure review the cause and remain silent until it is your time to speak.

Rules and Regulations

Keep yourself to yourself. If unconvinced, inform a senior member of the staff of how to prioritize they will then assist you in personal priorities.

Wear comfortable clothing and comfortable shoes at all times make sure that composure is kept.

Attend work early, on time or else arrive early for work at the correct time or time that's within reason of projects and tasks.

Conform to rules and regulations if an assignment you don't receive a brief alert a senior member of staff who will then issue you one.

Conformation of duties and changes must be made to the relevant personnel.

Irrelevant articles will be eliminated and reviewed if they are dispatched needlessly or if these harbor illegal content.

Abusive demeanor will be given formal warnings before filled for acquittal at all times remain polite toward the staff and yourself for company harmony and civilized purposes.

Paperwork and files are to be completed on time and handed to a senior personnel

Legislations
Obstruction
Copyrights
Legitimacy

Contract

Staff administration staff duties – apart from the main executive bosses and managers, the next main official is the administration, who files accounts slips and the rest of the financial data. As they secure this, they are the most relevant power body as staff duties require.

Staff duties include
- journalism/journalism media
- editing
- secretary staff
- office work/office duty
- technician – technical safety
- workplace efficiency
- marketing media
- management – employee maintenance
- staff well-being
- support assistance

All employees of Wuning will be hired and worked via the handout of briefs. Also, lectures will be held frequently as a company staff duty, so all must attend. Here people will be given routine assignments as part of their vocation. Assignments will be handed out to the staff from their hierarchy boss's on inductions depending on their chosen occupational and professional design such as their department. Briefs will be handed out during staff meetings for the work of joint projects, and people will be sent on assignments in groups, attending things such as seminars and auctions.

Staff meetings – will be held to inform occupants of the present project that they are projected to work on (usually in file with occupation).

The occupations are as follows, management duty will be working in the Wuning first department and participate in journalism as a manager. They will be expected to occupy themselves with managerial duties such as maintenance ordering staff. Administration duty occupation participation journalists they will be expected to occupy themselves with money management and account observation. Finance staff will listen to the chief administrator and work under her command. Logistics will have the main focus of journalism and the main power also they will produce direct, manage, write and survey off site areas as journalist. Their main participation is to work on surveys and ensure diagnostics are inserted and filed to the correct people. (Production duties pre-maintain the Wuning building is the company's hierarchy order). Occupation of the sho – gas staff will be too ensuring that everybody's leisure interest are taken care of and to liaise with the project manager frequently. Their subordinate duties are to cater to staff and ensure the caterers are taking care of health and safety. A sales representative for Wuning will have to network for marketing to distribute production merchandize. Their occupation is to get things sold on the media's markets. Secretary's occupation is to get in touch and answer phone calls for their department manager. Their main duty is to file papers and keep in touch with their management.

Expectations – The expectation of Wuning is to deliver films to the highest of quality and to a world class standard. Operating at the highest level to deliver unassuming material on time. The expectation of Wuning is to write, plan and produce high level scripts and quality entertainment features to a plentiful amount of twenty a year. Along with entertainment shows, cartoon, animations, children's television and quiz shows. Wuning will work and push to the highest of standards to compile quality and amusing entertainment to a vast and varied audience.

Roles – The roles of Wuning department is top priority business people to order the other four departments in management secretaries and leisure. Professional responsible staff of a commanding division will interact liaise and assign other staff to do their bidding which means arranging wages and following duty. Here they will produce and preproduce scripts writing to the finalization of scripts. Administrate commission and secretly discuss on files.

Pre-production – Production teams groups of nine writers will write analyze draft and coedit, scripts to a high standard. Management leads the four main departments apart from the five main executive posts. The personal assistant (PA) of the Wuning executive boss has full power of the company when his gone. (Managerial associate) Management in Wuning is to ensure the boss talks are met sufficiently.

Employees –
Preproduction – team of writers
Administration – team of secretaries
Management – liaise with writers ensure production maintenance of staff and departments
Security – stay in main office watching films and captions *Employment type*

EMPLOYMENT PROCEDURES

APPLICATION FORM –

Application forms are to be filled in by all new employees before joining. This will go on to a personal file and stack in the recruitment officers file–fax.

INDUCTIONS –

At staff inductions, all new employees will get a signed contract stating their chosen profession, occupations will be reviewed and evaluated.

LECTURES –

Staff will be held fortnightly at lectures to receive briefs and evaluations to assign new recruits and employees to their departments.

SEMINARS –

Hierarchies of employees will be expected to intend company seminars and displays lending insight into their work and profile.

DIAGNOSTICS –

Will be held frequently to decide on employee's literally and media level.

OCCUPATION BRIEFS -

Will be handed out to new recruits and employees monthly.

TERMS AND CONDITIONS OF EMPLOYMENT – Employment – profession occupation tasks

Arrival – on time

Attire – casual and comfortable

The end

Printed in the United States
By Bookmasters